MW01616682

THE DRUG ADDICT'S HANDBOOK

(FOR RECOVERY)

M.C. LEE

SECOND EDITION

This book contains the opinions and ideas of its author. It is intended to provide helpful general information on the subjects it addresses. It is not in any way a substitute for the advice of the reader's own physician(s) or other medical professionals based on the reader's own individual conditions, symptoms, or concerns. If the reader needs personal medical, or other assistance or advice, the reader should consult a competent physician and/or other qualified health care professionals. The author and publisher specifically disclaim all responsibility for injury, damage or loss that the reader may incur as a direct or indirect consequence of following any directions or suggestions in the book, or participating in any of the programs described in the book.

Published by Big Change Publishing, Mesa, AZ

The Drug Addict's Handbook (For Recovery)
2nd Edition ISBN-13: 978-1-7335763-3-8

For more information:
thedrugaddictshandbook.com
cellvention.org

Printed in the United States of America

Dedicated to those who
have found ways to help
addicts survive.

PREFACE

This little book contains everything I would say to folks while they were in the residential program I ran for five years in Scottsdale, Arizona. It was originally written for addicts in jail, who may have had to cope with going through withdrawal in a difficult place. So often we have no money, no insurance, no job, no skills, no hope, and nobody by the time we are ready to change.

Many addicts in this country will not have access to treatment. Many small towns have no treatment facilities and for a lot of addicts, obstacles to getting treatment anywhere include lack of money or insurance to pay for it.

I am glad if you are able to get clean using any method. If church works, or medication or psychiatry—anything at all—I am happy for you. But for many addicts none of these were sufficient to get clean and stay clean.

The suggestions I am making in this little book are intended to help you make a start in recovery. If you find a better approach, or invent one yourself, I think that's great. But use what's available to get your recovery rolling. There are resources that are free, and available that can help you get started.

My hope is to distribute thousands of these little books to jails all over the country, and to other settings where addicts have limited access to treatment. I want to make this information available to any drug addict thinking about getting clean. To offer everyone the same information that people paid a thousand dollars a day for in treatment.

I am not suggesting there are no advantages to being in a treatment program—treatment can be incredibly helpful—but I am suggesting you work with what you have available. Use what has worked for others and then pass that on if you can. Your experience can save lives.

I hope you find the happiness and peace of mind you are searching for. That thing the drugs gave us in the beginning, before they chewed up our lives.

M.C. Lee

THE DRUG ADDICT'S HANDBOOK

CHAPTER ONE:

THINKING ABOUT GETTING CLEAN

You can do
whatever
you want.

This is
your life.

You do not
have to
stop using.

No one will
ever be able
to make you
stop using.

As long as
we think
someone else
is the reason
we use, we will
never get clean.

We can't control
other people.

We use because
we want to use,
or because we
have to use.

We use because
we can't stop
using.

We might have started using because of the behavior of other people, but we don't continue to use because of them.

No one has the power to stop us from using or to keep us using.

You will
stop using
when you
want to.

You can
stop using,
as unlikely
as that might
seem.

It definitely
can be done.

Anyone can
stop using.

The trick
is staying
stopped.

Honesty can be
hard, but that is
where recovery
begins.

If I don't think I
am an addict,
I am not going
to do the work
of recovery.

If the diabetic
doesn't think
they have diabetes,
they are not going
to do the work that
requires: watching
their diet, checking
their sugar and
taking their
medication.

People are
confused about
what addiction
is. It is not
the physical
addiction to the
drug (although
that is certainly
part of it for
some addicts).

It is the way
we think.

And the way
we think is not
transformed
when we get
clean.

It takes a lot of
time and effort
to change the
way we think.

No drug will ever
help us see the
world more clearly.

That is why there
will never be a drug
to cure addiction.

As long as
we think that
drugs are the
solution, we
will continue
to use.

The bad
stuff that has
happened will
not keep you
clean.

It helps us to
get started but
then it drifts off
into the past and
loses its power.

We need to
think about
what we want.

Happiness?
Peace of mind?
Family? Career?
Health? Money
in the bank?
True friends?

These are goals
that can wake
up with us every
morning.

That don't drift
off into the past.

What do
you want
out of life?

Why would
you want to
stop using?

What bad things
would stop
happening?

What good
things could
happen?

What would
the payoff be?

What would
have to change
to stop using?

Drugs changed
how we saw the
world but did
not change the
way things were.

The next day we
got up and still
had the same
life we had
blotted out.

Recovery offers
us a chance to
change the way
things are.

Addicts tend to
see the worst
possible outcome
in their minds
when looking out
into the future.

Recovery helps
us to see other
possibilities.

Every addict is
a rebel without
a pause.

We have a lot
of difficulty
taking direction
from others.

What you tell yourself, the words that you use, can cause big problems.

When you tell yourself you should do this or must do that, you may rebel even though no one else is involved.

Try to
remember
that you
are free.

You don't
have to do
anything.

You make
the decision
to get clean.

But then you
need to do
something.

Chapter Two:

Getting Clean

Not using
drugs is the
key to change.

As long as you
use, you will
not change.

Get whatever
help you can
with detox,
but not every
addict is going
to have help.

Jail can be a
great place
to stop using
(even if there
are some drugs
there).

Many addicts
have found
recovery in jail.

ICU can be a
great place to
stop using.

Running out
of drugs or
money can
be a great
time to
stop using.

Actually
anytime is a
good time
to stop using.

For the most
part addicts
are not
dying from
withdrawal,
they are dying
from using.

If you get the
opportunity to
get into any
kind of treatment
program, no
matter how great
or how wacky
it is, stay for the
whole program.

Maybe
one in a
hundred
addicts stay
clean when
they leave
treatment
early.

You want
better odds
than that.

Treatment
improves
your odds
of success.

But treatment
is not magic.

Each of us
has to do the
work of early
recovery to
stay clean.

You are not
going to feel
good for a
while, either
physically or
emotionally.

The body
takes a while
to heal.

If you have
to feel good
immediately
after you stop
using, you are
not going to
stay clean.

The positive
experiences
we have
with drugs
leave strong
memories.

People and
places that are
a part of those
memories are
huge triggers
for relapse.

We need
to distance
ourselves from
those triggers,
as much as we
can, or go
back to using.

We ask for
help in so
many ways.

I can't build
a car, grow
my own food
or generate
electricity.

I need help to
do all these
things.

But addicts
hate to ask for
help when it
comes to their
addiction.

If you do not
ask for help,
you will not
stay clean.

When I ask
for help with
my addiction, or
my emotions, I
risk that person
not coming
through for me.

And that
would hurt.

Addicts want
more than
anything not
to get hurt.

But we
have to risk
getting hurt
to get better.

Someone may
let me down,
but in 12 step
fellowships,
the group will
probably come
through for me.

The 12
steps are
a path to
successful
recovery.

We need
a path to
follow.

There is a
pretty good
chance I am
not going
to invent
another path.

I would not
have any idea
how to do
that.

If you are in jail or prison, take advantage of any meetings that the 12 step fellowships bring into the facility.

The addicts
who do those
meetings
usually have
a lot to offer
and they aren't
asking for
anything in
return.

The more
you attend
meetings,
anywhere,
for any
reason, the
better your
chances of
getting clean.

No matter
what brings
you to a
meeting, you
are able to
hear people
talking about
recovery, and
some of that
might stick.

I have known addicts who went to meetings with a court card, saw the opportunity recovery offered and took it.

Anyone can.

If you do
everything
you can to get
better, you'll
be fine.

If you don't
do everything
you can, you
will probably
go back to
using.

Some of us
are able to
get into a
treatment
program,
and some of
us aren't.

Some of us
have access
to hundreds
of meetings,
and some
have access
to only a few.

Attend as
many as
you can.

12 step
meetings
are not all
the same.

Each fellowship,
AA, NA, CA,
CMA and
HA all have
different
cultures.

They all have a
different feel.

Each of
the 12 step
fellowships
has a history.

Alcoholics
Anonymous
is the oldest
and was
started in
1935.

Narcotics Anonymous started in 1953. Cocaine Anonymous started in 1982, Crystal Meth Anonymous started in 1994 and Heroin Anonymous started in 2004.

Each of
the 12 Step
fellowships
was started
to serve a
different
group of
addicts.

Each of them
has developed
meetings,
literature and
a culture, that
is different
from the
others.

You need
to find the
fellowship
where you
feel at home.

The key to using 12 step meetings to stop using, and stay stopped, is finding the culture that you can relate to.

And sticking around long enough to get it.

The first
three steps
in the 12 step
fellowships
are the key to
getting clean.

In the first step we admit we are not able to pull this off by ourselves.

In the second step we accept the idea that there is something that can help us succeed.

In the third step we decide to accept that help, and put it into action.

You do not
have to believe
in God to get
clean in a 12
step fellowship.

Some addicts
use the term
Higher Power
as another
name for what
is needed.

Something
bigger than
you that
can help
you succeed
in recovery
is what they
are talking
about.

The 12 step
fellowship
or the
meetings
can function
as a Higher
Power.

You decide
what it is.

You need help
and the 12 step
fellowships can
help: they have a
clear set of
steps to follow,
supportive addicts
in recovery and
books that explain
what has worked
and what has not
worked for them.

The word
God appears
repeatedly in the
steps and in the
literature.

Many addicts
think of that as
Good Orderly
Direction.

Don't get
stuck on the
word God
and miss
all the ideas
around it.

When we
first get
clean, we
may not
have any
structure
in our lives
at all.

Meetings
provide some
structure.

Something
to build the
rest of it
around.

Something
that we know
is going to
happen each
week on a
regular day
at a regular
time.

Attending
meetings
every day
is a wise
move at the
beginning.

The Drug Addict's Handbook

Most addicts
were using
drugs every day.

A meeting takes
an hour or two
but it might be
the only time in
the day when
you are focused
on how to stay
clean.

Often addicts have attended one or two meetings and decided that it was not going to work.

The meetings might have been terrible, and the people might have been wacked.

Those few
meetings are not
the fellowship.

There are some
wonderful
meetings in
all of these
fellowships.

You need to
find them or
start them.

When you find
a meeting you
enjoy, ask people
what other
meetings they
are going to.

There is a good
chance you will
enjoy those too.

Anyone can
start a 12 step
meeting.

Each of the
fellowships will
provide the help
needed to start
a new meeting.

If you are
not finding
meetings
that work for
you in your
area, start
one.

Every meeting
is different.

Each one has a
different crowd,
a different room
and different
format.

You do not
have to stop
using to go
to meetings.

I have known people who attended meetings for years, never able to stop, or stopping and relapsing many times, and then got clean.

If you aren't hitting people or flipping tables over, you should be welcome at meetings.

The only requirement for membership is a desire to stop using.

Twelve step
meetings
are free.

They pass a
basket to pay
the rent, but
you do not
have to throw
anything in.

A sponsor
is basically a
mentor.

Someone
who knows
something
about recovery
and is willing
to help you to
recover.

Sponsors
are not
magic.

They have
problems
themselves
and may fail
you in some
way, but they
can offer
support that
can be a
lifesaver.

Members of
the 12 step
fellowships
understand
anger and
have had their
own anger
problems.

They are not
afraid of your
anger like most
people are.

When we
go to 12 step
meetings
we will find
some troubled
people.

The whole idea
is to attract
troubled people
so they can get
better.

I am always
amazed when
people are
surprised to
find some
knuckleheads
at meetings.

Meetings are
one of the
few places
that an addict
can be a total
knucklehead
and people
will say "Keep
coming back."

It can be
hard to trust.

In active
addiction
we surround
ourselves
with people
who are not
trustworthy,
and neither
are we.

The Drug Addict's Handbook

But we need
to begin to
trust, in small
ways at first,
if we are
going to be
successful in
recovery.

At meetings,
you get all
the secret
knowledge
the first day.

Then you have
to practice
it for it to be
useful.

If you hand
a man who
wants to
become a
carpenter a
toolbox filled
with tools,
that does not
make him a
carpenter.

He needs to practice using them, and it helps to do an apprenticeship where someone with the skills teaches him how to use the tools.

We need to
be open to
new ideas.

What we
know when
we first get
clean is not
going to help
us succeed.

We know a lot about using.

We need to open our minds to new ways of thinking, new ways of acting and new ways of seeing the world.

You need to create safety around you.

Constant stress or folks who are using are going to move you back toward using.

Calm places
and folks who
are not using
are going to
help you move
forward in
recovery.

Family members are not able to provide an addict with the help they need.

There is too much emotional baggage.

Family members
tend to bring up the
past and get angry,
or enable us to keep
using, or cut us off
and provide no
support.

None of those
things are very
helpful when we
have fifteen
minutes clean.

To put some
distance between
you and the
people you have
been close to in
active addiction,
does not mean
you will never
be close to them
again.

Living with a
using addict
is probably not
going to work out.

I have only known
one addict who
lived with using
addicts and stayed
clean.

Odds are way
against you.

If you hang
out in the
barber shop,
you are going
to get a haircut.

If you hang out
with folks who
are using, you
are going to
use.

You do not
know what is
going to happen
if you relapse.

We think we
know, but we
don't.

Usually bad things
happen that we
are not expecting.

It takes 90 days
to start thinking
more clearly after
you get clean.

It takes much
longer to really
function at 100%.

If you are willing
to hang in and
stay clean, you'll
get there.

The body has
an amazing
ability to heal.

The brain has
an amazing
ability to heal.

I knew a
woman who
was beaten
badly when she
was using and
could barely
walk or talk
when she got
clean.

Years later she
was doing fine.

Most of us
have not done
nearly that much
damage in active
addiction, and we
too can heal.

To be accepted
and respected
just the way
you are, that
is such a rare
thing for an
addict.

You will
find that at
meetings.

Recovery is
like riding a bike
uphill.

You either keep
pedaling or you
roll backwards.

Or you fall over.

You can get
clean and
stay clean.

If our future
was determined
by our past
experience,
no one would
get clean.

We can
learn from our
experience and
do something
different.

CHAPTER THREE:

STAYING CLEAN

Addiction is a
chronic illness,
like diabetes.

It requires daily
care to stay
healthy.

THE DRUG ADDICT'S HANDBOOK

Like diabetes,
you need to
make changes in
your life in order
to stay healthy.

For diabetes it is
changing what
you eat, checking
your sugar and
taking your
medications.

For addiction
it is not using,
changing who
you hang out
with, where
you hang
out, staying
connected
with others in
recovery and
working on
change.

You are
changed
by what
you do,
not by
what you
think.

There are many ways that people have stopped using drugs, but there is no way for me to know which one you might discover.

Friends,
family, church,
medicine, school,
psychiatry,
reading self-help
books and many
other things I
am unaware of
might help some
addicts get clean.

But for any
individual
addict, we can
only discover
what that was
after it happens.

12 step recovery offers a clear path that has worked for many, and after all these years working with addicts it still seems like the best path to suggest to get started.

If you are
able to find
an alternative
that works
for you, I am
delighted.

With 12 step
recovery, you
get the experience
of others, places to
meet regularly
to talk about
recovery, people
to work with on
the challenges of
staying clean,
and literature
that helps explain
how to do it.

At meetings
there are
opportunities
to help others,
which can help
us to feel better
about ourselves.

There are
many benefits
of recovery
in 12 step
fellowships.

Recovery is like
college.

You can intend
to get a degree.

You can want to
get a degree.

But to actually
get a degree
you have to
sign up, go to
classes, study,
take the tests
and then sign
up for the next
semester.

You have to be
willing to do
the work.

Recovery does not mean you will not have problems.

Life presents all of us with problems, along with the good stuff.

Recovery is about learning how to deal with problems without the use of drugs.

We create
most of our
own problems
in active
addiction and
in recovery.

You are not
going to be
able to save
the people
you care
about when
you first get
clean.

There is a
tendency for
addicts in early
recovery to
want to try to
help friends
and family
stop using.

You are
more likely
to go back to
using than
they are to
stop if you
are spending
time with
them.

Your story
can save
lives.

If you are attending meetings, addicts will show up who are hopeless and sharing your story honestly—what it was like, what happened and how life is today—can be a powerful message of hope for the newcomer.

Helping
another addict
will help you
to get out of
thinking about
your problems,
your fears and
your regrets.

When the addict with two days clean welcomes the addict with 15 minutes clean at a meeting, the addict with two days gets some relief from their own thinking.

Helping
other addicts
get clean gives
us a purpose
in our lives.

Something to
build the rest
of our lives
around.

The kindest
thing you
can do for
the people
in your life
is stay clean.

If you stay clean, you never have to go through withdrawal again.

When people tell you the truth, there is a strong possibility you won't like it.

But the truth grows on you if you let it.

Secrets will
kill you.

One of the great
things about
the 12 step
fellowships is
that no matter
what you have
done, other
members of the
fellowship have
done it too and
they can relate.

The Drug Addict's Handbook

Many meetings
provide an
opportunity
for you to hear
someone who
just got clean
talk about how
things were
going while
they were using.

It is a powerful
reminder of
where we don't
want to go.

The 12 steps might sound difficult to work through, but they help addicts find some peace with the past and have less fear of the future.

The 12 steps help us to live in today, where we can actually do something with our lives.

The books
and pamphlets
each fellowship
has can be
lifesavers.

The experience of hundreds of addicts has been written down, and you have the opportunity to use that experience in your recovery.

You can
do this.

You can
recover.

And find the
happiness
and peace
of mind you
have been
looking for.

Appendixes

Who Can Help?
How To Start a Meeting
The Benefits of Meetings
Virtual Meetings
Literature Online
Resources

Appendix One:
Who Can Help?

You are going to want to identify who can help you to stay clean. Explore your options.

Any kind of substance abuse treatment would be helpful. Don't turn down any opportunity. I am convinced even the worst program is better than no program. Some are short term but some programs offer intensive outpatient programs that could help get you through the first few months of your recovery. We need some accountability. And treatment is a great opportunity to work on our rebellion.

Twelve step meetings can provide a lot of help, but in your area if there aren't a lot (or any) meetings, others might help you to build a community of recovering addicts. Anyone can start a meeting. The next appendix will describe how to start a meeting in each of the four large fellowships for addicts.

Local churches might be able to offer space for a meeting, or help you to locate others in the area who are in recovery. AA began with Bill W. looking for another alcoholic and asking the pastors of local churches for suggestions.

Finding another addict who is staying clean could be a blessing. You may have a family member or friend who got clean years ago who you have been avoiding while using drugs. You might want to seek them out. The two of you getting together in a coffee shop is a meeting. Meetings don't have to be formal. AA started out with alcoholics meeting for coffee.

You can't have a meeting until you have a second person. You need one more person to meet.

The police and courts in some small towns have developed programs to help addicts get into treatment, rather than jail. As addiction has taken a toll on their families and those of their neighbors, the people in law enforcement have become more open to trying to help addicts.

There may be a doctor in town who could help by prescribing non-narcotic medication to help with withdrawal. It would be worth asking.

Getting to a local AA meeting a half an hour early would give you the opportunity to ask if they know any other drug addicts in the area you could contact who are interested in recovery. It would also give you a chance to see if they are open to you attending the AA meeting if you don't have a history with alcohol.

AA members helped addicts form all of the other 12 step fellowships including NA, CA, CMA and HA.

Perhaps they could also help you get a meeting for addicts off the ground.

People you have been using with can help by giving you enough distance to get started in recovery. People who really care about you are going to be willing to stay away if that would help you to get clean, or stay clean. No one who is a true friend would offer you drugs if they knew you were trying to stop using. People who care about you will want to help you succeed, and not to undermine your efforts.

Your library might have 12 step literature. Some of the literature is available online and you can see it on your phone, or on a computer.

Take a healthy risk and ask for help. We took all kinds of risks in active addiction and we need to learn how to take healthy risks in recovery.

The Drug Addict's Handbook

APPENDIX TWO:
HOW TO START A MEETING

How to Start an NA Meeting:

Narcotics Anonymous was started in 1953 by a few addicts in Van Nuys, California who had been attending AA meetings. It grew very slowly and at times nearly disappeared. One man, Jimmy K. kept the fellowship alive for many years, working out of the trunk of his car. It grew in the 1970's and 80's until in 2016 there were more than 67,000 NA meetings in 139 countries. Narcotics Anonymous is focused on the disease of addiction rather than on specific substances. There are members who have used every drug of abuse including: pills, heroin, cocaine, alcohol, marijuana and methamphetamine. NA meetings can be found in every large metropolitan city and many small towns.

On the Narcotics Anonymous World Services web site NA.org click on For Our Members, click on How To Start A Meeting in the drop down menu and then follow the instructions. They can help you start a meeting in your area and literature can be downloaded for free. The phone number for the Services Team is 818-773-9999 extension 771.

How to Start an C.A. Meeting:

Cocaine Anonymous was started by AA members in Los Angeles in 1982 hoping to start a meeting where they could apply the 12 steps and their shared experience to their cocaine addiction. C.A. is a very inclusive fellowship. Most C.A. members have a history of addiction to stimulants, but that is not a requirement for membership. In 2016 there were 3000 C.A. meetings worldwide.

On the home page CA.org, click on Meetings. On that page click on Yes You Can Start a C.A. Meeting under Further Information. You can download meeting formats and also request a C.A. meeting starter kit back on the Meetings page.

How to Start a CMA Meeting:

Crystal Meth Anonymous was started in 1994 in Los Angeles by an AA member who had recovered from the use of crystal meth and had 16 years clean. He wanted to have a fellowship where members could share freely about their crystal meth addiction. In 2016 they had 600 meetings in the US and Canada and six other countries.

On the home page crystalmeth.org, click on CMA Meetings, then click on START A MEETING, then download the starter materials. The meeting guidelines, formats and pamphlets are free online.

How to Start an HA Meeting:

Heroin Anonymous was started in Phoenix, Arizona in 2004 by AA members who had successfully recovered from heroin addiction.   Again the fellowship was started to give heroin addicts a place to focus on the 12 steps and their addiction to heroin.

On the home page heroinanonymous.org click on Resources and on the next page meeting formats and readings are available for download. To inquire about starting a meeting, and to request a meeting start up kit send an email to hastartupkits@gmail.com or write them at HAWS, 24 W Camelback Rd #A, Phoenix, AZ 85013.

THE DRUG ADDICT'S HANDBOOK

Appendix Three:
The Benefits of Meetings

There are a variety of benefits to be gained when the newcomer chooses to begin attending meetings and some of those are listed below.

Asking for help: One of the most important skills that the newcomer to recovery can develop is that of asking for help. Meetings provide opportunities to practice asking for help, to develop that skill.

Literature: The NA Basic Text was released in 1983. The experience of those recovering in NA was captured in one place for the benefit of members. Each of the 12 step fellowships has literature that describes the process of recovery. A lot is known about recovery and it has been written down.

Celebrating Clean Time: To most people, staying clean for thirty days is not very impressive. The folks at work, or the neighbors, or often times the family would look a bit puzzled at someone announcing that they had not used drugs, including alcohol, for 30 days. At meetings people get pretty excited about that—and the celebration of recovery is fun.

Human Contact: One of the harsh realities of addiction is isolation.   Meetings are a place where the addict seeking recovery can begin to experience human contact. That contact may be physical, expressed through handshakes or hugs. It may be eye contact, looking another person in the eye without fear of being judged or rejected. The contact might be through conversation, allowing others in recovery to begin to know them. It may simply be a shared laugh or smile.

Folks Who Do What You Want to Do: For many people new to recovery, one of the greatest concerns is that they will not be able to do those things that they have enjoyed doing, that are associated with their active addiction.   Those activities may include hunting and fishing, bowling, baseball, watching football on TV—activities associated with the use of drugs including alcohol. The reality is that there are many folks attending meetings that share those interests – whatever they are.

Learning What Does Not Work in Recovery:
There are a lot of things that really don't work in recovery—ways of thinking and behaving. Those things that don't work are revealed at meetings by those attending as they share their experience. This represents a tremendous opportunity for those interested in succeeding in recovery. They learn what mistakes to avoid from folks that have made them.

A Place to Talk About What's Going On:
There are opportunities at meetings to talk about the difficulties of the day and the feelings you are having. Folks often need these opportunities on a regular basis in early recovery and there is no more appropriate place to talk about those challenges. Before, during or after the meeting.

Social Activities: What to do after you stop using is a question many have when they first enter recovery. There is often a belief that there is no fun after one begins to abstain, and known entertainment options are most often related to using alcohol and other drugs. The reality is that there is an entire world of recovery entertainment and activity for the newcomer, and the most effective place to plug into it is at meetings.

Getting Equal: Meetings are a place where folks can begin to see that they are "one of" a larger group of people experiencing similar problems. This concept is addressed in the 12th tradition of the 12 step fellowships. It is critical to successful recovery, that the newcomer recognize that they are suffering from the same problem as their peers and that the same solutions that are working for others will work for them.

Experience: What is needed most in early recovery is experience. The most important experience needed is having the desire to use drugs, and not using. There are a range of other experiences that are critical in recovery. It is possible to benefit from the experience of others with more time in recovery, and they are found at meetings.

Facing Fears: Fear drives a lot of behavior in active addiction—fear of facing the past, the present and the future. Facing fears is a big part of recovery and meetings provide opportunities to do that. The only way that folks in recovery make any progress working through their fears is by taking the risks and facing them. Through facing fears, they are overcome—and life itself becomes less frightening. The meetings are a safe and supportive place to begin that process.

Making New Friendships: The key to building relationships is shared experience. As folks enter recovery, it is frequently important to put some distance between themselves and friends they have had in active addiction. At meetings, they are able to meet others facing a similar challenge—who are seeking to live life without the use of drugs.

A Place to Identify as an Addict: In order to stay focused on the need for all of the work involved in recovery, those new to recovery must stay aware of the problem that they are trying to address. Each time they attend a meeting, and introduce themselves as an addict, they reaffirm their belief that they have the disease of addiction, and that they believe the solution lies in working the 12 steps.

Finding Identification: Finding identification with others sharing a common problem is a powerful experience. I know something is wrong. I am convinced that my problem is unique. I do not know what the solution is. Then one day I walk into a 12 step meeting, and suddenly things change dramatically. Listening to others speak about their experiences, I know what my problem is. I am no longer unique—and I have discovered a solution.

Making Mistakes: Meetings are one of the few places in the world where you can make a total fool of yourself and folks say "Keep coming back." Newcomers to recovery need opportunities to make mistakes, without paying the penalties associated with saying or doing the wrong thing. Meetings provide a proving ground for developing social skills in recovery and those new to recovery need that opportunity.

Part of a Larger Fellowship: There is a larger fellowship beyond the individual meeting, and the meeting functions as a gateway. In local areas there may be many meetings, even hundreds in large metropolitan cities. The reach of the fellowships of Narcotics Anonymous, Cocaine Anonymous and the other 12 step fellowships is much further than that. The larger fellowships are worldwide societies of recovering folks. When an addict becomes a member of the local fellowship, they also become a part of this network that touches all parts of the globe. It is by attending the meetings that we become aware of this larger world of recovery, and the opportunity to find like-minded people wherever we go.

Perspective: One of the most difficult aspects of recovery is the tendency of addicts to see their lives in a distorted way. There is a tendency toward negative evaluations of life events, or black and white thinking. There are too few grays. Perhaps most importantly, those with the disease of addiction are frequently wrong about what is happening. Hearing the perspective of others helps the newcomer to come back to a more accurate assessment of their situation.

A Place to Practice Principles: Honesty is a great concept, a terrific principle. It is also extremely difficult for folks new to recovery to practice in their lives. All of the principles that underlie the 12 step programs can be difficult to achieve. It is said that Honesty, Open-Mindedness and Willingness are the principles that members absolutely cannot ignore. It takes a lot of practice to develop these abilities and much of that practice can occur at meetings.

Repetition: In early recovery, it can be difficult to hear what is being said, to see what is right in front of us, and to acquire the tools needed to build a successful life after drugs. Repetition is the key to our recognizing and retaining those insights and tools. When members tell newcomers to keep coming back to the meetings, they reveal a fundamental truth, without repeated exposure to various events at meetings, members are unlikely to "get it."

Responsibility: There is a great line in the NA Basic Text: "Through our inability to accept personal responsibility we were actually creating our own problems." Meetings are the place that the newcomer can begin to experiment with being responsible, to themselves and others. The first experiment might be with taking responsibility for personal recovery. It is not possible for anyone to give recovery to another. Each individual seeking recovery has to gain their own experience, and a large part of that is taking responsibility for doing the kinds of things that contribute to recovery. A number of those can be done at meetings.

A Safe Place: For the addict who has been using drugs, the world can appear a hostile place, filled with risks and temptations to return to old patterns of behavior. In many ways the world of the newcomer is hostile to the idea of their changing. Meetings are a safe place in that hostile world, and a place where the focus is on recovery rather than using. Meetings offer a way to escape those pressures, and a safe haven where the newcomer can surround themselves with others who have a desire to stay clean.

Self Esteem: There are two essential elements for the development of feelings of self-worth:

successfully completing the tasks we set for ourselves, and the esteem of others. Opportunities for both of these are available at meetings. Recovery is in fact a series of actions. When the newcomer forges ahead and completes the tasks that support recovery, they feel better about themselves. The other piece of this is the esteem of others. Meetings are a rare place where people demonstrate that they care about the addict. And for many addicts, this is the only place they will encounter this concern.

Service to Others: Being of service to others is one of the suggestions found in recovery in 12 step fellowships. Early in the history of 12 step recovery, it was recognized that those who made an effort to carry the message of recovery to others stayed clean. Service efforts help the newcomer, and the old-timer, to get out of self-obsession. The meetings offer various opportunities to be of service to others, both formal and informal.

Social Skills: 12 step Meetings offer continuous opportunities to develop and hone social skills. Frequently, those attending meetings have developed skills based on the use of substances, have developed skills only useful within a subculture, or have failed to develop social skills at all. Many of the skills that were useful in active addiction prove useless in recovery. Basic abilities in areas like friendship, conversation, and relationships may be lacking, and meetings provide countless chances to practice them. This is an unusual opportunity. We can make a lot of mistakes and people keep saying "We'll love you until you love yourself" or "Keep coming back."

Public Speaking: For most of the folks entering recovery, public speaking is the last thing on their minds and you do not have to speak at a meeting. Addiction is an isolating problem and just talking to another person, one on one, may well be a challenge. The structure of the meetings in the 12 step fellowships is such that folks gain the ability to share honestly what is going on with them. This is the most important skill in recovery. And the fear of speaking in public disappears for most of us.

Sponsor: A sponsor is someone who can help the newcomer to recover through the 12 steps. The sponsor is a mentor, with personal experience recovering. Individual sponsors vary widely in what they do or don't do. They may help the person seeking recovery to work through the steps quickly, or they may just be a willing listener at the beginning. They may be very directive, clearly instructing the person seeking recovery on what they need to be doing, or very loose and informal in their approach. Whatever approach a sponsor takes, the easiest place to find one is at a meeting.

The Twelve steps: For many, learning about the 12 steps is a key activity one becomes involved in at meetings. These steps, which provide a new perspective on life as well as a series of concrete actions toward a more productive way of living, originated in Alcoholics Anonymous and have been adapted by NA, CA and other fellowships. There are several ways in which attending meetings helps the individual seeking recovery to better understand and apply the principles underlying the steps. It is an opportunity to hear the steps read aloud, to hear the experience of others working the steps, and to express your own personal understanding. There is no better place to be learning more about the steps.

The Still Suffering: It is possible to be of service to others in all areas of our lives. The individual seeking recovery, however, is challenged by the 12th step to carry the message to the still suffering addict. The message is that recovery is possible. In order to do that you have to have some still suffering addicts available, who have an interest in recovery. Those folks can be found at meetings.

Structure: The use of drugs drives the activities of active addiction. When folks first come to recovery, they are often lacking events around which to structure their new lives. Where once it was stopping at the bar after work, now there is a void. Where once it was the search for more drugs, now there is a void. Many are jobless, isolated, and without non-using friends to spend time with. Meetings provide structure in a productive and consistent way. Once the newcomer has identified meetings that are appealing, they know where they will be at that time on that day of the week. They are then able to structure their lives around this framework of meetings.

It Works: There are a lot of folks successfully recovering. It is hard to identify who those people are in our everyday lives. Walking down the street, you can't distinguish who is recovering from those who are not. Meetings are one of the rare places where you can actually find a group of folks who are succeeding in recovery—and it becomes clear that people do recover. Until newcomers get to meetings, most are aware of only one or two people in recovery. Some are aware of none. At meetings it is quickly revealed that many individuals have made a comeback from the depths of addiction, and that provides hope.

So meetings offer much more than is immediately apparent. Not only do they provide a range of important benefits to those seeking recovery, but they are free (a basket is usually passed to pay rent and for supplies, but no donation is required) and for many addicts the meetings are readily available. Give yourself a break and take advantage of this opportunity. You have nothing to lose, and a great deal to gain.

APPENDIX FOUR:
VIRTUAL MEETINGS

In March of 2020, for the first time ever, many 12 step groups around the world were unable to meet in person. There have always been times that addicts were unable to gather together for a meeting: natural disasters, the facility closing or the group getting kicked out due to our behavior. But there had never been anything like the Covid-19 pandemic.

Meeting with others to work together was always a part of the solution to addiction. Going back to the earliest days of Alcoholics Anonymous, folks met at each other's homes to drink coffee and support each other through the challenges of recovery. Suddenly in March of 2020, gathering together became dangerous because of Covid-19. Many facilities where addicts met closed: community centers, churches, clubs, restaurants and other settings.

We were told by public health officials that no more than 50 people and then no more than 10 people could gather together in one place. There had to be at least six feet between all of the people and there were to be no handshakes or hugs. People needed to wear masks or face coverings. Physical contact with other addicts had been a feature of recovery from the beginning. Now for most of us that stopped. This was a huge loss for many addicts and for many of us it was the biggest challenge we had faced in recovery.

Fortunately there was some technology to help. If you got clean in 1985, all the technology available was landline phones and phone booths. There were no cell phones. There was no internet. No Facetime or Skype or Zoom. Today nearly every addict can access a phone that allows you to call another addict, no matter where you are or where they are. This is an incredible tool in recovery.

There had been online or phone meetings for years, but most addicts had never attended them because there wasn't a need. When you can attend face to face meetings safely, you tend to favor that. It is simple and there is nothing like a bunch of recovering addicts sharing and laughing together. But suddenly, in a matter of days, we needed something else. Virtual meetings became that something else and we were glad to have it.

Virtual meetings make some things possible that never were possible. Addicts can attend meetings in other parts of the country and other countries without leaving home. We are able to really get a sense of how big the recovery community is and how diverse we are. And the meetings are still free.

Thousands of online meetings were started. The NA, CA, CMA and HA fellowships all started a lot of virtual meetings. Groups that were unable to meet started a virtual one to replace that meeting. At ten o'clock on Monday morning, there was now an online meeting by the same name, that group members could attend. Addicts and groups of addicts started additional virtual meetings and this happened all over the world. Suddenly the addict in Chicago could attend a meeting in New York, or Miami or England. The options expanded.

One of the advantages of face to face meetings is that the addict only has to walk in to benefit. Virtual meetings present some challenges to getting there in the first place. And you have to get there to get the benefit. Thinking about getting there will not work. So addicts using virtual meetings have to be willing to learn, to persist and experiment until online meetings are practical.

With face to face meetings, addicts also have to learn, persist and experiment. When addicts first show up for face to face meetings, the whole experience is new. The format of the meetings is a mystery. Recovery in 12 Step fellowships is a mystery. Most of the people there are strangers and the whole experience can be, and frequently is, awkward. Many of these challenges are the same with online meetings.

But in addition the addict is faced with some technical challenges. How to log into the meeting. Downloading the software if necessary. Knowing how to participate. How to see the other addicts who are attending. How to raise your hand. How to mute the microphone on your phone or computer. But if we are willing to learn, persist and experiment, all of these challenges can be pretty easily overcome. This is far from impossible. Just new and different.

I think the biggest challenges are the same ones we face with all meetings. Finding the meetings that we enjoy is at the top of the list. As with all meetings, virtual meetings are all different. Different formats. Different crowd. Different feel. Different focus. Some meetings are filled with laughter and some are grim. Look for the laughter.

It is helpful if you can find meetings online that folks in your area are attending. Then you can begin to build relationships and support in your community. You want to find meetings where people are talking about how they use the solutions provided by 12 Step fellowships. Folks who are honest about the challenges and the successes in their daily lives. Who care. Who want you to succeed.

The usual ways that addicts with time in recovery help newcomers can be more challenging in virtual meetings. Frequently at face to face meetings, they would offer encouragement and phone numbers after the meeting. This happens at virtual meetings too, but often a number of people are talking and it can be hard to isolate your conversation. It is even more important for newcomers to attend meetings regularly to connect with others, to ask for phone numbers before or after the meeting, and to call other recovering addicts outside of meetings to get the support they need early in recovery.

Helping the newcomer is an important part of the program. Folks with some time clean want to help. And members of all the 12 step fellowships are using the phone more often and really want to hear from newcomers. This old technology has become more important than ever. Remember to leave a message if they don't pick up so they can call you back. Everybody has become more skeptical of phone numbers they don't recognize.

I believe the simplest way to get started is to attend Zoom meetings. The technology may well change in the future, but currently the whole world seems to be using Zoom to stay in touch. The software is free and the virtual meetings of all of the fellowships serving drug addicts are largely on the Zoom platform. NA, CA, CMA and HA all have links on their fellowship home page to a list of virtual meetings.

The Zoom application is available for free for Android and iPhone and for Windows and Mac computers. You can download the Zoom App for your device on the Zoom.us website. On the home page click on Resources at the top and scroll down to Download Zoom Client. For computers, either PC or Mac, click on the Zoom Client for Meetings button. For Android or iPhone, click on either the Google Play or Apple App Store for Zoom Mobile Apps further down the page. Once you have downloaded Zoom, you can click on a link for a meeting found on an online fellowship meeting list and the Zoom App will open. Type in the Passcode if there is one and you're in. Or you can open the App and type in the correct meeting ID and Passcode. You might want to write that information down for meetings you enjoy.

Video is optional (a black screen with your screen name will appear instead of video) and your microphone is usually muted unless you are participating. You can see all the participants in a grid on the screen or just the speaker.

You don't have to participate and with the video turned off, no one is going to see you. This gives you an opportunity to explore with absolutely no risk of having to do anything. This is also something you don't get at face to face meetings, where as you would expect, people are going to see your face. As usual some meetings are closed meetings for addicts only and some are open meetings where anyone can attend. That information is found in the description.

Details could change as the technology evolves, but this should give you a running start.

Virtual Meeting Links

Narcotics Anonymous: Go to the NA.org home page. Click on For Our Members at the top and click on Virtual Meetings in the dropdown menu. Down that page is Find a Meeting in red. Click on Virtual-na.org. Look for Zoom in the meeting link.

Cocaine Anonymous: Go to the CA.org home page. Click on Meetings at the top of the page and scroll down to Online Meetings. On the Online Meetings page click on the day of the week. Look for Zoom in the meeting link. You can also download an online meeting list on that same page.

Crystal Meth Anonymous: Go to the Crystalmeth. org home page. Click on CMA meetings at the top of the page and scroll down to Online/Hybrid CMA Meetings. On that page, select a day of the week, choose a meeting from that list and look for a Join with Zoom button on the meeting information page.

Heroin Anonymous: Go to the HeroinAnonymous. org home page. Click on Covid-19 in the menu bar at the top of the page. On the Covid-19 page, click on Click Here for a List of Online Meetings and look for Zoom in the meeting link.

Appendix Five:
Literature Online

Each of the four large fellowships serving drug addicts have literature available online. This is an incredible resource. Years ago the only way you could read the pamphlets describing aspects of the program was to order them or pick them up at a meeting. This is an example of how technology is helping people to recover from drug addiction. These can be read on a phone or a computer. Check out the library if you don't have access to a computer.

Narcotics Anonymous: All of the pamphlets and booklets are available to be read online or downloaded from the NA.org web site. Start on the About Us page, click on download literature on the next page, click on Recovery Literature on the next page, select a language and then click on the link for the literature you want. A lot of information about recovery from addiction is free on the web site.

Cocaine Anonymous: CA also has all of its pamphlets available online to read or download from the CA.org web site. On the home page click on Literature and on the next page click on whichever pamphlet you have an interest in. They currently have over 25 pamphlets available online covering a wide range of CA related topics. There is a lot that you can learn about recovery from addiction in CA on the Cocaine Anonymous web site.

Crystal Meth Anonymous: CMA has all of their fellowship pamphlets available to read online or download from their web site crystalmeth.org On the home page click on For the Fellowship and click on CMA literature in the dropdown menu. The next page has download buttons for the pamphlets. There are currently over 15 pamphlets available that you can download explaining various aspects of recovery in CMA.

Heroin Anonymous: HA has eleven pamphlets on their web site. To get to the page with the pamphlets, on the home page click on Literature and then click on the Read More for each of the pamphlets. Great resource.

Appendix Six: Resources

Narcotics Anonymous:

NA World Services
PO Box 9999
Van Nuys, California USA 91409
Telephone 1-818-773-9999
Website: NA.org

Cocaine Anonymous:

CA World Services Office
21720 S. Wilmington Ave., Ste. 304
Long Beach, CA 90810-1641
Telephone: 1-310-559-5833
Website: CA.org

Crystal Meth Anonymous:

CMA General Services
4470 W. Sunset Blvd. Suite 107 PMB 555
Los Angeles, CA 90027
1-855-638-4373
24 Hour Helpline 855-METH-FREE
Website: crystalmeth.org

Heroin Anonymous:

Heroin Anonymous World Services
24 W Camelback Rd #A
Phoenix, AZ 85013
heroinanonymous.org

The Recovery Book (2014)
by Al J. Mooney M.D. Catherine Dold, Howard Eisenberg, Workman Publishing

(available from Barnes and Noble, Amazon and other outlets)

The Recovery Book is a great overview of the challenges faced by addicts in recovery and the variety of resources available. This book is used as the basic text for many treatment programs.

NA Basic Text, 6th Edition

(available from Narcotics Anonymous World Service Office and other outlets)

Written by addicts in NA sharing their experience working the program and members' stories.

Hope, Faith and Courage, 2nd Edition

(available from Cocaine Anonymous World Services Office and other outlets)

Written by members of CA with the fellowship history and members' stories.

Recovery Speakers.com

This is a web site that has recordings of 12 Step speakers dating back to the beginning of recovery in AA. There are Narcotics Anonymous speakers, Cocaine Anonymous speakers and Heroin Anonymous speakers telling their stories or talking about their experience of their fellowship. This gives the newcomer a chance to hear someone talking about their recovery and can help to demystify the fellowship. The quality of the recordings varies and the older the recording the rougher the quality.

Substance Abuse and Mental Health Services Administration

SAMHSA (Substance Abuse and Mental Health Services Administration) National Helpline: 1-800-662-HELP (4357). SAMHSA's National Helpline is a free, confidential, 24/7, 365-day-a-year treatment referral and information service (in English and Spanish) for individuals and families facing mental and/or substance use disorders

THE DRUG ADDICT'S HANDBOOK

About the Author

The author is a Licensed Clinical Social Worker who has been working with drug addicts and alcoholics for over 30 years. For five of those years he was the Program Coordinator for the Villa residential chemical dependency program at Banner Behavioral Health Hospital in Scottsdale, Arizona. As an administrator he has also been the Director of Outpatient Services at a psychiatric hospital. Over the years he has worked with addicts at every level of substance abuse treatment including: detox, day treatment, intensive outpatient, family groups and individual therapy. In addition the author has done thousands of mental health and substance abuse evaluations. Clients have included addicts from all walks of life, including men and women, young people and the elderly, the homeless and the wealthy, members of the military, and those with other medical or emotional problems.

Special thanks to John C. whose support made this book possible.

Made in the USA
Middletown, DE
09 September 2021